Rose Elliot's Book of Savoury Flans and Pies

Rose Elliot is the author of several bestselling cookbooks, and is renowned for her practical and creative approach. She writes regularly for the *Vegetarian* and has contributed to national newspapers and magazines as well as broadcasting on radio and television. She is married and has three children.

Ferguson

Other titles available in the series

Rose Elliot's Book of Beans and Lentils
Rose Elliot's Book of Breads
Rose Elliot's Book of Cakes
Rose Elliot's Book of Fruits
Rose Elliot's Book of Pasta
Rose Elliot's Book of Salads
Rose Elliot's Book of Vegetables

Rose Elliot's Book of
Savoury Flans and Pies

Fontana/Collins

First published in 1984 by Fontana Paperbacks,
8 Grafton Street, London W1X 3LA
Second impression January 1986

Copyright © Rose Elliot 1984

Set in 10 on 11pt Linotron Plantin
Illustrations by Ken Lewis
except page 3 by Vana Haggerty
Made and printed in Great Britain by
William Collins Sons & Co. Ltd, Glasgow

Conditions of Sale
This book is sold subject to the condition
that it shall not, by way of trade or otherwise,
be lent, re-sold, hired out or otherwise circulated
without the publisher's prior consent in any form of
binding or cover other than that in which it is
published and without a similar condition
including this condition being imposed
on the subsequent purchaser

Introduction

Delicious flans with creamy fillings and crisp pastry, flaky golden pies, melt-in-your-mouth tartlets: everybody loves them and they're useful for so many occasions, ranging from picnics and informal suppers to parties and special dinners. In this book I have given what I hope are foolproof instructions for making the most useful types of pastry, followed by a varied collection of recipes for using them, to make all kinds of tasty savoury dishes.

TYPES OF PASTRY

The types of pastry which are useful for savoury flans, pies and tartlets are shortcrust, cream cheese pastry, which is a flaky version of shortcrust, and three different traditional flaky pastries: flaky, rough puff and puff. The same basic ingredients and equipment are used for all these pastries; the difference lies in the proportions of the ingredients and the way in which they are combined.

INGREDIENTS FOR PASTRY

Flour Plain flour gives the best results. 100 per cent wholewheat flour makes a tasty, healthy shortcrust pastry, just right for chunky flans and homely pies. For a lighter, more delicate shortcrust, and for flaky pastries, an 81–85 per cent wholewheat flour gives excellent results, and for puff pastry, unbleached white bread flour.

Fat Butter, margarine, lard or cooking fat can all be used. For shortcrust pastry I use either polyunsaturated margarine, which makes very good pastry, or half butter and half white polyunsaturated vegetable fat which you can buy from supermarkets.

Liquids A little cold water is needed to bind the ingredients together; egg yolk can also be used to bind shortcrust pastry, giving a particularly light, flaky result. Lemon juice is added to flaky pastries to improve the elasticity of the gluten in the flour.

Other ingredients Grated or cream cheese can be added to shortcrust pastry, also flavourings such as herbs, chopped nuts, grated lemon rind, curry powder and other spices to complement the filling used.

EQUIPMENT

The equipment for pastry-making is simple and basic. You will need some scales, a sieve and a large mixing bowl, also a clean dry surface on which to roll out the pastry. If you can get one, a marble slab is ideal, as this helps to keep the pastry cool, but you can use a clean working surface or, as I do, a large pastry board. It's also useful to have a pastry brush for dampening the edges of pies with water and for glazing. I prefer a traditional bristle pastry brush with a wooden handle.

When it comes to plates, tins and dishes for flans and pies, metal is generally the best material as it conducts the heat well and helps to make the pastry crisp. You will need a baking sheet: get the heaviest and strongest you can find; a flan tin with a removable base: the 20-cm (8-in) size is the most useful; and a 1-litre (1½–1¾ pint) pie dish with a wide rim. Some little flan dishes or tins measuring 10 cm (4 in) across and 1 cm (½ in) deep are pleasant to have, but not essential, as is a tartlet tin with 12 shallow, rounded hollows for making small pies.

MAKING THE PASTRY

When following a pastry recipe it is important to note that the quantity stated always refers to the weight of flour from which the pastry is made, not the total weight of the finished dough. So 200 g (8 oz) pastry means pastry made from 200 g (8 oz) flour. It's particularly important, too, when following pastry recipes, to stick either to metric or imperial measures, because in order to keep the correct proportions of ingredients there may be more discrepancy than usual between the metric/imperial equivalents.

Shortcrust Pastry

This is the easiest pastry to make and the most useful.

MAKES 200 G (8 OZ) PASTRY

200 g (8 oz) plain flour
½ teaspoon salt
50 g (2 oz) butter
50 g (2 oz) white vegetable fat
8 teaspoons water (approx.)

Sift the flour and salt into a bowl. If you're using wholewheat flour, sift through as much flour as you can, then add the residue of bran from the sieve (the purpose of the sifting is to aerate the flour, not to remove the bran). Add the butter and fat, then rub them into the flour with your fingertips, lifting the mixture high out of the bowl to incorporate as much air as possible and make the pastry light. Continue until the mixture looks like fine breadcrumbs, then add the water a little at a time and use your fingertips to press the mixture together and form a dough. Put the dough on a lightly floured surface and knead lightly for a minute or two until smooth. If there's time, wrap the dough in polythene and chill for 30 minutes in the fridge. This relaxes the dough and makes the pastry easier to roll out, but isn't essential. Before rolling out the dough, use your hands to press it roughly into whatever shape you want – a round, oval or rectangle – then roll out using light, even strokes and bake in a hot oven, 200-220°C (400-425°F), gas mark 6–7.

Cheese Shortcrust

Make this as shortcrust opposite, sifting ½ teaspoon mustard powder with the flour and adding up to 50–150 g (2–5 oz) grated cheese after rubbing the fat into the flour. Bind with cold water or 1–2 egg yolks.

Cream Cheese Pastry

This is the easiest way I know of making a pastry with a flaky texture; it is a most delicious pastry, at its best when made with an 81 per cent or 85 per cent wholewheat flour, although it is the one flaky pastry which also works with 100 per cent flour. Suitable for pie crusts, savoury rolls and tartlets.

MAKES 200 G (8 OZ) PASTRY

200 g (8 oz) plain flour
½ teaspoon salt
100 g (4 oz) butter or polyunsaturated margarine

100 g (4 oz) full fat cream cheese
1 teaspoon lemon juice

Make as for shortcrust pastry, adding the cream cheese and lemon juice after you have rubbed the fat into the flour. Chill for 1 hour before using; bake as for shortcrust pastry.

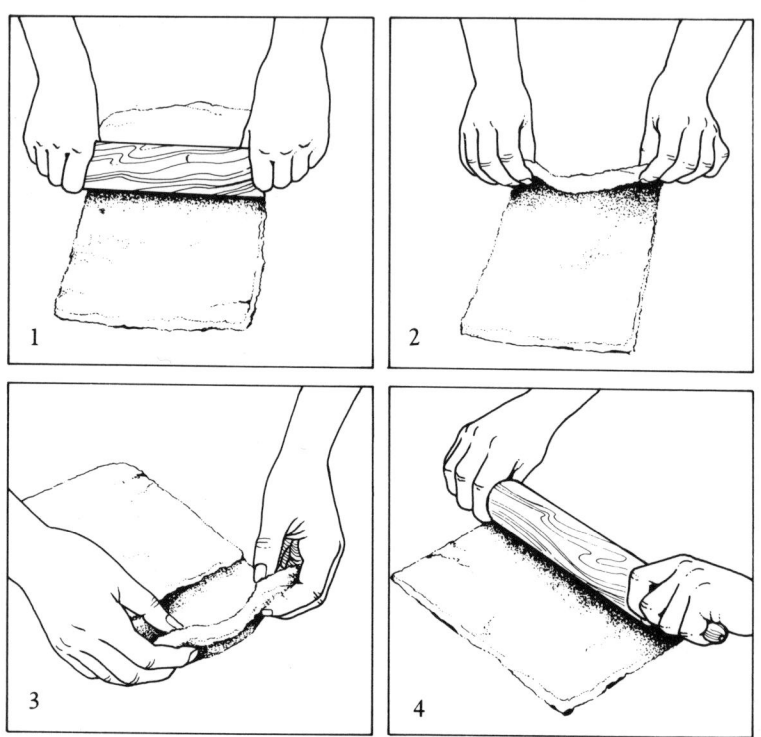

Rough Puff Pastry

This is the quickest and easiest of the traditional flaky pastries and a good choice for savoury rolls and decorated pastries. Lightest when made with white flour, it also works well with an 81 per cent or 85 per cent wholewheat flour, which is what I normally use.

MAKES 200 G (8 OZ) PASTRY

75 g (3 oz) butter or hard margarine
75 g (3 oz) white cooking fat
200 g (8 oz) plain flour
½ teaspoon salt
2 teaspoons lemon juice
6 tablespoons cold water (approx.)

Cut the butter or margarine and fat into walnut-sized pieces and chill in the fridge. Sift flour and salt into a bowl. Add fat, cutting it in lightly with a round-bladed knife so that the fats get coated with the flour and are about the size of a pea. Then add lemon juice and water. Using your fingertips, gently gather the mixture together to form a soft pliable dough. Put the dough on to a lightly floured surface and, without kneading, shape to a rectangle. Roll out to an oblong three times as long as it is wide (about 12 x 36 cm/5 x 15 in), see figure 1 on page 10. Fold the bottom third up and the top third down, as shown in figures 2 and 3 (page 10), then lightly press the edges together with the rolling pin (figure 4). Give the dough a half turn so that the open edges are at the top and bottom, then roll out to a long strip again and repeat the folding and sealing. Wrap the dough in polythene and chill in the fridge for at least 30 minutes, then repeat the rolling, folding and sealing twice more and chill for a further 30 minutes. Rough puff pastry should be baked in a hot oven, 200–220°C (400–425°F), gas mark 6–7.

Flaky Pastry

This is the flakiest pastry apart from puff and ideal for making special pies. This way of making flaky pastry is based on the one described by Claudia Roden in *A Book of Middle Eastern Food*. It is a highly unconventional method but, having tried them all while testing recipes for this book, it is the one which I have found gives best results every time, rising in delicious flaky layers, even with 81 per cent wholewheat flour.

MAKES 200 G (8 OZ) PASTRY

200 g (8 oz) plain flour
½ teaspoon salt
150 g (6 oz) butter, at room temperature

2 teaspoons lemon juice
8 tablespoons cold water (approx.)

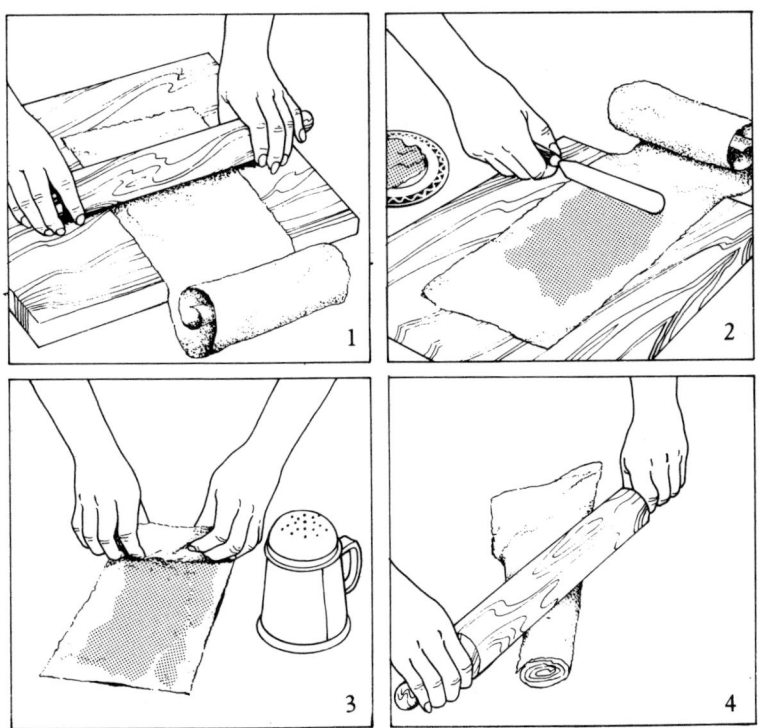

Sift flour and salt into a bowl and rub in 50 g (2 oz) of the butter. Add the lemon juice and enough water to make a pliable dough. Wrap in polythene and chill overnight in the fridge. Next day form the dough into a rectangular shape and roll it out as thinly as possible. You will have a very long piece of pastry and will need to fold up the part you've already rolled or allow it to hang over the pastry board while you work on the rest (see figure 1 on page 13). Next spread the surface of the dough evenly with the rest of the butter, as in figure 2, then roll the dough up like a swiss roll (figure 3). Wrap the roll of dough in polythene and chill in the fridge for 1 hour. Then roll out the pastry as shown in figure 4 and use as required. Bake in a hot oven, 200–220°C (400–425°F), gas mark 6–7.

Puff Pastry

This is the flakiest pastry of all and is used for vol au vents and occasionally as a topping for pies. It is quite time-consuming to make, though not difficult if you work methodically. It's a good idea to chill the bowl you're going to use, the flour and the water and lemon juice before you begin. This pastry does not work satisfactorily with wholewheat flours; when I make it for the occasional treat I use an unbleached white flour. The quantities given in the recipe are based on a 250-g (9-oz) block of butter.

MAKES 250 G (9 OZ)

250 g (9 oz) unbleached plain flour
1 teaspoon salt
8–9 tablespoons water
1 tablespoon lemon juice
250 g (9 oz) unsalted butter

Sift the flour and salt into a bowl. Add the water and lemon juice and mix to a dough. Turn on to a lightly floured surface and knead a little, then wrap in greaseproof paper and a damp cloth and chill for 30 minutes. Meanwhile take the butter, put it between two pieces of greaseproof paper and, using first your hands and then a rolling pin, press it to a rectangle 10 x 15-cm (4 x 6-in). Chill. Put the chilled dough on to a lightly floured working surface and roll out to a circle about 30 cm (12 in) across. Put the rectangle of chilled fat in the centre of the circle and lift the edges of dough over it, as in figure 2 on page 15, so that the fat is enclosed in the dough. Turn the rectangle so that the short edges are at the sides, and roll out, as in figure 3. Roll gently in one direction only, until the pastry is double its size. Then fold the bottom third of the pastry up, and the top third down over that (figures 2 and 3). Seal the edges with the rolling pin (figure 4), page 10. This all constitutes the first rolling. Next wrap the dough in greaseproof paper and a damp cloth and chill for 15 minutes. Then put the dough on to the lightly floured surface

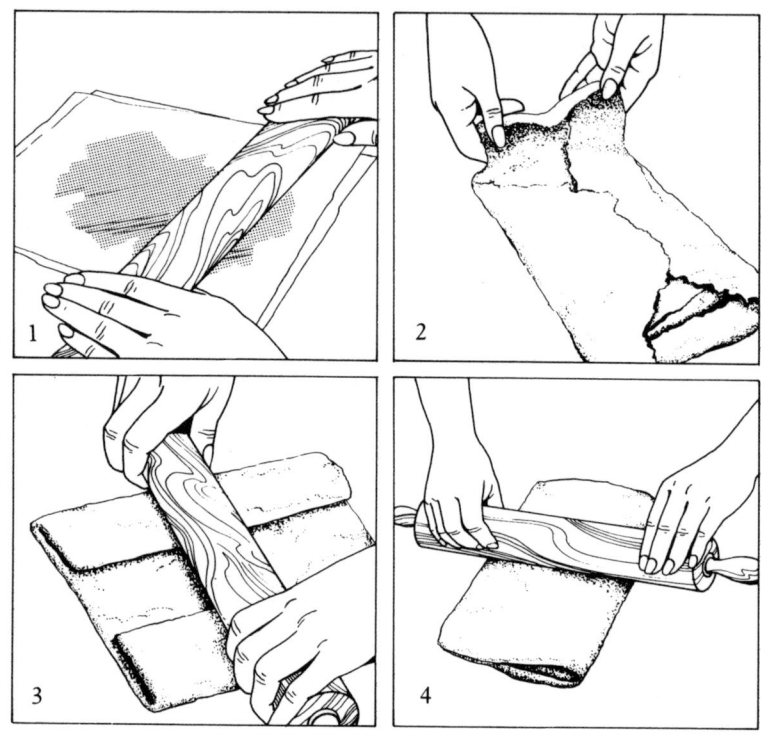

with the longest edges at the sides (figure 4), and roll out and fold as before, then chill again. Repeat this process four more times, until the dough has been rolled and rested six times in all. Then wrap the pastry in greaseproof paper and a damp cloth and chill for at least 2 hours before use. Puff pastry should be rolled out fairly thickly and baked on a damp baking sheet in a hot oven, 200°C (400°F), gas mark 6.

MAKING A SINGLE-CRUST PIE

First prepare the filling, as it needs to be completely cooled. To make the pastry lid, pat the pastry out to roughly the shape of the dish, then roll it out 6 mm (¼ in) thick and about 1.5 cm (½ in) wider all round than the top of the dish (figure 1, page 18). Cut a strip from the outer edge of pastry and place on the rim of the dish. Put filling into dish and if it's moist and soft, stand an egg cup in the centre of the dish to help support the pastry. Damp the pastry strip on the rim with cold water, then place the pastry on top as shown in figure 2 on page 18 and press the edges together. 'Knock up' the pie and flute the edges as in figure 3 on page 18, then insert the blade of a knife under the pastry at the sides of the pie to make a gap for the steam to escape, or make a couple of steam-holes in the top of the pie (figure 4). Decorate with pastry trimmings as desired (page 21) and brush top of pie with beaten egg or milk to glaze, if you wish.

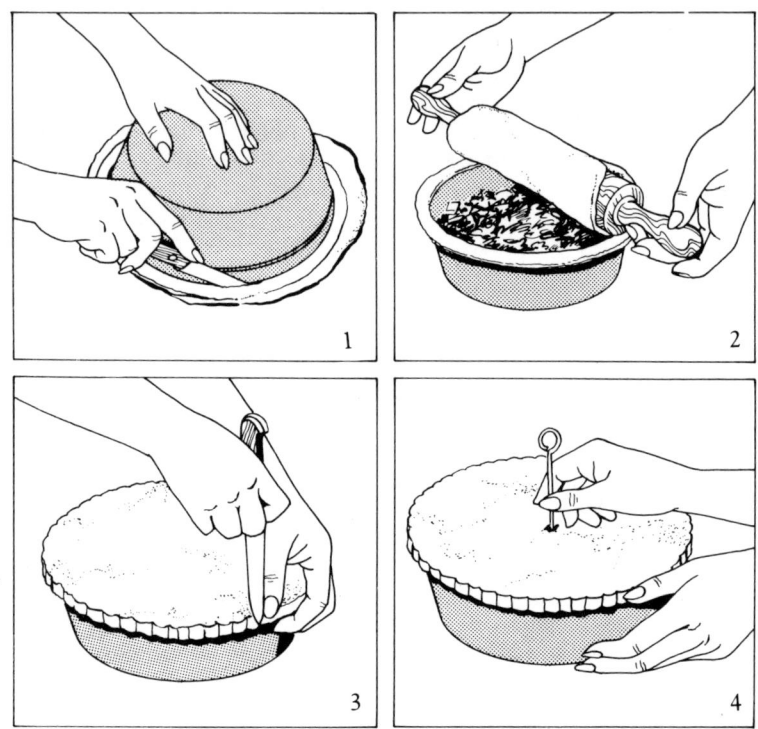

MAKING A DOUBLE-CRUST PIE

Prepare and cool the filling. Take just over half the pastry, pat into the shape of the dish and roll out about 3 mm (⅛ in) thick and about 2.5–4 cm (1–1½ in) larger than the dish. Lift pastry into dish, press into place, then spoon the filling in on top: it should fill the dish generously, piled up to the centre. Roll out remaining pastry so that it is 1 cm (½ in) larger than the dish, then place on top of dish to cover filling. Press pastry edges together, trim, knock up, decorate and glaze just as described for single-crust pies and shown on page 21.

MAKING QUICHES, FLANS AND TARTS

Set the oven to 200°C (400°F), gas mark 6, position oven shelf above centre and place a large baking sheet on the shelf. Lightly grease a flan tin. Roll out the pastry fairly thinly so that it is 4 cm (1½ in) wider all round than the diameter of the tin. Then lift it into the tin, using either the rolling pin or, and this is easier with crumbly wholewheat pastry, sliding it straight off the pastry board into the tin. Press pastry into tin, trim edges, prick base. When making an ordinary shallow flan I do not think it is necessary to weight the pastry down with baking beans; just put flan tin into oven on top of baking sheet (which helps to cook base of flan) and bake for 15–20 minutes, until pastry is set and feels crisp and firm when you touch it lightly. If you want to ensure that your flan has a lovely crisp base, just before you take the flan case out of the oven, heat 2 tablespoons of oil in a small saucepan. Tip oil into flan case as soon as it comes out of the oven. You can then continue and put the filling straight in on top, or leave the flan case to get cold before proceeding. Either way this tip, which was discovered by a friend of mine, means you will never make a soggy flan again!

It's fun to experiment with different combinations of ingredients for the filling. Although cream is often used – and is wonderful for a special occasion – lower calorie versions can be made by using milk, half milk and half single or soured cream, or by substituting a low-calorie soft white cheese such as fromage blanc or quark.

FREEZING PASTRY DISHES

Double-and single-crust pies freeze well. Freeze before baking, then thaw completely and bake the usual way. You can freeze flans but I do not think they are satisfactory as the pastry is never as crisp. It is better to bake the flan case and freeze it without the filling; it doesn't take long to whisk up a filling later, and this can be put straight into the frozen flan case and baked normally. Recipes which are suitable for the freezer are shown by the symbol Ⓕ

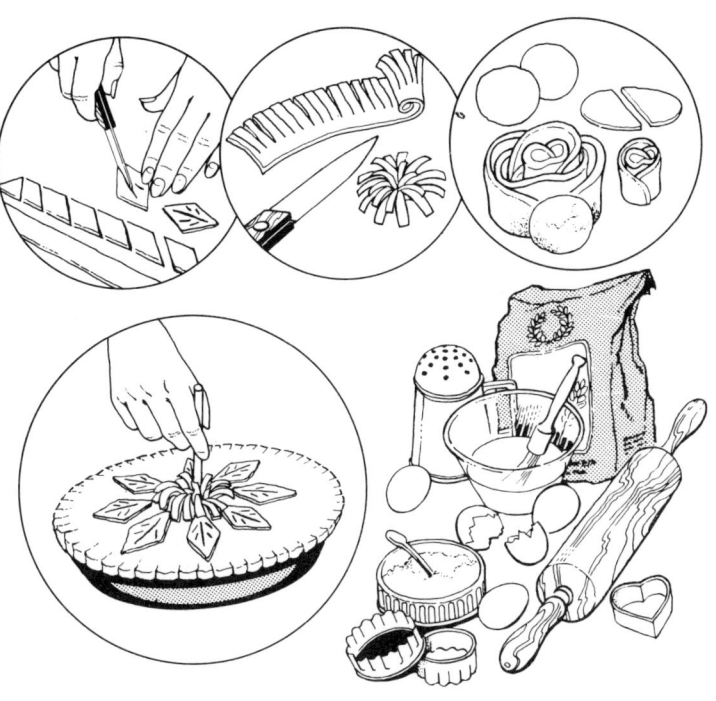

Little Avocado Flans

With their melt-in-the-mouth pastry and delicate avocado topping, these make a delectable first course.

SERVES 6

150 g (6 oz) shortcrust pastry
2 tablespoons oil
25 g (1 oz) butter
25 g (1 oz) flour
275 ml (10 fl oz) milk
1 teaspoon mild mustard
50 g (2 oz) grated cheese
salt and pepper
2 avocado pears
3 tablespoons lemon juice

Set oven to 200°C (400°F), gas mark 6. Roll out pastry and line six 10-cm (4-in) tartlet dishes. Bake as explained on pages 19-20, adding hot oil to baked flan cases as described. Melt butter in a saucepan, add flour, cook for a moment then pour in milk, stirring until thick. Add mustard and most of cheese; season to taste. Peel and dice avocados, sprinkle with lemon juice, gently stir into sauce. Divide between flans, sprinkle with rest of cheese. Bake for 15–20 minutes.

Little Flaky Brie, Walnut and Sorrel Pies

Serve these hot from the oven as a delicious first course; or accompanied by salad, made from diced eating apples and tomatoes, watercress and a little finely shredded leek, for a light lunch.

MAKES 12

150 g (6 oz) flaky, rough puff or cream cheese pastry
125 g (4 oz) Brie, finely diced
25 g (1 oz) walnuts, chopped
25 g (1 oz) sorrel or spinach, finely shredded
salt and pepper

Set oven to 220°C (425°F), gas mark 7. Roll out pastry and cut out 24 circles with a 6-cm (2½-in) round cutter. Place 12 of these in a lightly greased tartlet tin. Mix together Brie, walnuts and sorrel or spinach; season lightly. Divide mixture between tartlets, cover with remaining circles, press edges together. Make a steam-hole in the centre of each little pie, then bake for 15 minutes, until crisp, golden brown and flaky looking. Serve at once.

Butter Bean, Onion and Chutney Roll

Quick to make, economical and nourishing, this is good hot or cold, and useful for packed lunches.

SERVES 4 (F)

2 onions, sliced
2 tablespoons oil
125 g (4 oz) butter beans, soaked and cooked, or a 439-g (15½-oz can)
salt and pepper
100 g (4 oz) shortcrust pastry
2–3 tablespoons chutney
beaten egg to glaze

Fry onions in the oil for 10 minutes, until soft. Drain butter beans; add beans to onions, together with salt and pepper. Leave on one side to cool. Set oven to 200°C (400°F), gas mark 6. Divide pastry in half; roll out each half to a rectangle about 26 x 22 cm (10 x 9 in). Place one rectangle on a baking tray, spread with the chutney, spoon bean mixture on top. Dampen edges with water, cover with second rectangle, press edges together. Brush with glaze, prick with a fork. Bake for 25–30 minutes.

Carrot, Courgette and Parsley Flan

A pretty mixture of colours in this summery flan.

SERVES 4—6

125 g (4 oz) shortcrust pastry
2 tablespoons oil
1 onion, chopped
175 g (6 oz) carrots, diced
25 g (1 oz) butter
175 g (6 oz) courgettes, sliced
150 ml (5 fl oz) single cream or milk
1 egg
2 tablespoons chopped parsley
salt and pepper

Set oven to 200°C (400°F), gas mark 6. Roll out pastry and bake a 20-cm (8-in) flan case as described on page 19, pouring in the hot oil as explained. Meanwhile fry onion and carrot in the butter, without browning, for 10 minutes, then add courgettes and cook gently for a further 5–7 minutes, until vegetables are tender. Spoon into flan case. Whisk cream with egg, parsley and seasoning. Pour into flan case. Reduce oven setting to 190°C (375°F), gas mark 5. Bake for 30–35 minutes.

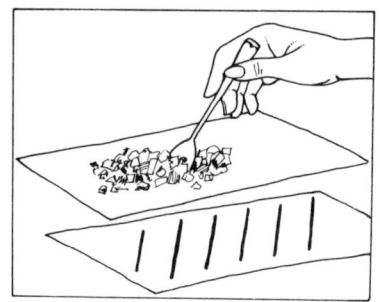
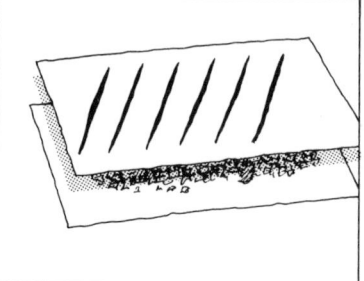

Flaky Cabbage, Rice and Hardboiled Egg Roll

Based on a Russian recipe, this is good served with a sauce made by stirring chopped herbs into soured cream.

SERVES 6

- 1 onion, chopped
- 25 g (1 oz) butter
- 350 g (12 oz) cabbage, shredded
- 125 g (4 oz) button mushrooms, washed and sliced
- 350 g (12 oz) cooked brown rice
- 4 tablespoons chopped parsley
- 2 hardboiled eggs, chopped
- salt and pepper
- 200 g (8 oz) rough puff or cream cheese pastry
- beaten egg to glaze

Fry onion in the butter for 5 minutes; add cabbage and mushrooms, cook for a further 10 minutes, until cabbage is tender, then add rice, parsley, hardboiled eggs and seasoning. Cool. Set oven to 220°C (425°F), gas mark 7. Roll half pastry into an oblong 26 x 22 cm (10 x 9 in). Spoon rice mixture on top, dampen edges. Roll out second half, cut as shown on page 28, place on top, press edges together. Brush with glaze. Bake for 35 minutes.

Cauliflower, Stilton and Walnut Flan

SERVES 4-6

125 g (4 oz) shortcrust pastry
2 tablespoons oil
1 small cauliflower
25 g (1 oz) butter
25 g (1 oz) flour

275 ml (10 fl oz) milk
125 g (4 oz) Stilton cheese, grated
salt and pepper
50 g (2 oz) chopped walnuts

Set oven to 200°C (400°F), gas mark 6. Bake a 20-cm (8-in) flan as described on page 19, adding hot oil after cooking as explained. Break cauliflower into florets, boil or steam for 5–7 minutes until just tender, drain. Melt butter in a saucepan, add flour, cook for a few seconds, then pour in milk and stir over heat to make a smooth sauce. Simmer gently for 5–10 minutes, to cook flour, then remove from heat, mix in 75 g (3 oz) of the cheese and season. Add cauliflower, stirring gently to coat. Spoon into flan case, sprinkle with rest of cheese and the walnuts. Return flan to oven for 30 minutes, until golden brown. Serve at once.

Cheese and Onion Pie

This pie makes a warming family meal, served with a homemade tomato sauce and vegetables.

SERVES 6 (F)

450 g (1 lb) onions, sliced
salt
200 g (8 oz) shortcrust, flaky or cream cheese pastry
225 g (8 oz) grated cheese
freshly ground black pepper
milk or beaten egg to glaze

Cook the onions in boiling salted water until just tender: about 10 minutes. Drain well, cool. Set oven to 220°C (425°F), gas mark 7. Roll out half the pastry and place in 1-litre (1½–1¾ pint) pie dish. Mix onions with cheese and seasoning, spoon on top of pastry. Moisten edge of pastry with cold water. Roll out rest of pastry to cover pie, press edges together, knock up as shown on page 18 and trim if liked (see page 21). Brush with glaze if you want a shiny finish, then bake for 30–35 minutes until pastry is crisp.

Cheese, Apple and Sage Turnovers

These are quick to make and have a moist filling with a pleasant combination of flavours. They are delicious made with <u>wholewheat pastry</u>.

SERVES 4 (F)

200 g (8 oz) shortcrust pastry
125 g (4 oz) eating apple, finely chopped
125 g (4 oz) grated cheese
1 tablespoon chopped fresh sage, or 1 teaspoon dried
beaten egg to glaze

Set oven to 200°C (400°F), gas mark 6. Divide pastry into four, roll each into a circle 15 cm (6 in) across. Mix together apple, cheese and sage. Place a quarter of the cheese mixture on one side of each piece of pastry, fold rest of pastry over and seal edges as shown on page 32. Brush with glaze, prick. Place turnovers on baking sheet and bake for 20–25 minutes, until golden brown and crisp.

Quick Cheese and Tomato Flan

If you put a simple filling straight into an unbaked pastry case, the flan can be on the table in an hour and although the pastry isn't as crisp as when it's pre-baked, the flan is tasty and delicious eaten hot with a cooked vegetable or salad.

SERVES 4–6

125 g (4 oz) plain wholewheat flour	175 g (6 oz) grated cheese
pinch of salt	2 eggs
50 g (2 oz) butter	150 ml (5 fl oz) milk
1½ tablespoons water	salt and pepper
	1 tomato, thinly sliced

Set oven to 190°C (375°F), gas mark 5. Make pastry as described on page 8, roll out pastry, line a 20-cm (8-in) flan tin. Sprinkle with the grated cheese. Whisk eggs and milk, add seasoning. Pour over cheese, then arrange tomato on top. Bake flan in centre of oven for 45–50 minutes, until set, puffed up and golden brown. Serve at once.

Little Curd Cheese Pies with Spicy Tomato Sauce

These little pies, with their creamy white filling, crisp wholewheat pastry and tangy tomato sauce, make a wonderful first course.

SERVES 6 (F)

200 g (8 oz) wholewheat shortcrust pastry
250 g (9 oz) curd cheese
garlic clove, crushed
salt and pepper

1 onion, chopped
2 tablespoons oil
450 g (1 lb) tomatoes, skinned and chopped
¼–½ teaspoon chilli powder

Set oven to 220°C (425°F), gas mark 7. Roll out pastry, stamp into 24 6-cm (2½-in) rounds, place half in shallow bun tin. Mix curd cheese with garlic and seasoning, then divide between tartlets. Place remaining circles on top, press together. Make a steam-hole in the top of each pie, then bake for 15 minutes, until crisp and golden brown. Meanwhile make the sauce; fry the onion in the oil for 10 minutes, add the tomatoes and chilli powder. Liquidize, season and reheat. Serve with the pies.

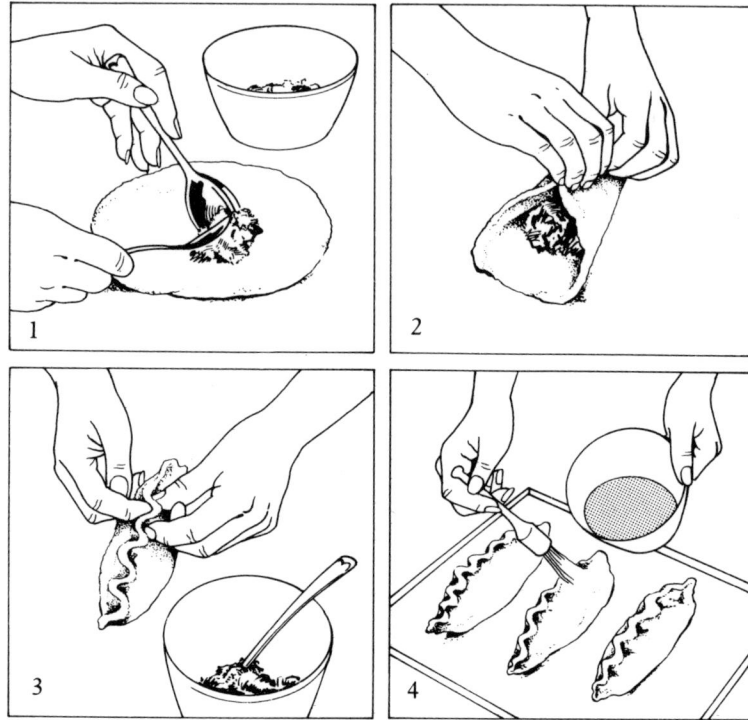

Spiced Chick Pea and Potato Pasties

MAKES 4 Ⓕ

1 onion, chopped
2 tablespoons oil
225 g (8 oz) potato, peeled and
  cut into 6-mm (¼-in) dice
1 tablespoon ground coriander
1 teaspoon ground cumin

125 g (4 oz) chick peas, soaked
  and cooked, or a 439-g
  (15½-oz) can
salt and pepper
200 g (8 oz) shortcrust pastry
beaten egg to glaze

Fry onion in oil for 5 minutes, then add potato and spices. Cook gently, covered, for 10–15 minutes, until potatoes are just tender, stirring often. Drain chick peas and add to potato mixture, season to taste. Leave on one side until cool. Set oven to 200°C (400°F), gas mark 6. Divide pastry into four pieces; roll each into a circle 15 cm (6 in) across. Spoon a quarter of chick pea mixture into centre, fold up pastry and press together edges as shown on page 36. Brush with glaze, then place on baking sheet; bake for 20–25 minutes.

Leek Lattice Flan

This is made in a square tin, to accommodate the shape of the leeks; the flan can be cut before serving and the squares arranged on a warmed plate.

SERVES 6

200 g (8 oz) shortcrust pastry
3 tablespoons oil
8 thin leeks, washed and trimmed
salt and pepper
300 ml (11 fl oz) soured cream
2 egg yolks
1 tablespoon chopped parsley

Line a 20-cm (8-in) square tin with pastry, cut trimmings into long strips, wrap in foil. Bake flan as described on page 19, adding hot oil after baking. Trim leeks to fit flan, then cook them whole in boiling salted water until tender: 15–20 minutes. Drain well, arrange side by side in flan case, sprinkle with salt and pepper. Whisk cream with egg yolks, parsley and seasoning, pour over leeks. Arrange reserved pastry strips in lattice over top, as shown on page 38. Reduce oven setting to 190°C (375°F), gas mark 5. Bake flan in centre of oven for 35–40 minutes, until set.

Leek Pie

Thick cream is traditionally used for this delicious Cornish pie. Thinking of all those calories, I make a lighter version, which is also excellent.

SERVES 4–6

1 kg (2¼ lb) leeks	150 ml (5 fl oz) single cream
salt and pepper	2 egg yolks
150 g (6 oz) flaky or puff pastry	milk or beaten egg to glaze

Wash and trim leeks, cut into 1-cm (½-in) lengths. Boil in salted water until just tender: 20–30 minutes. Drain well, season with salt and pepper, place in a 1-litre (1½–1¾ pint) pie dish and leave to cool. Set oven to 220°C (425°F), gas mark 7. Roll pastry, place on top of pie dish but do not dampen edges. Trim and finish as described on page 31. Bake pie for 25 minutes until crust is golden brown and crisp. Reduce oven setting to 170°C (325°F), gas mark 3. Remove pie from oven, slip knife under crust and carefully remove. Whisk cream with egg yolks and seasoning, pour over leeks. Replace crust and bake for further 25 minutes.

Lettuce, Pea and Spring Onion Flan

A most delicious blend of flavours and textures; serve with a fresh tomato salad for a light summer lunch.

SERVES 4-6

125 g (4 oz) shortcrust pastry
2 tablespoons oil
6 spring onions, chopped
½ lettuce, shredded
125 g (4 oz) shelled fresh peas or frozen petit pois
25 g (1 oz) butter
6 sprigs mint, chopped
150 ml (5 fl oz) single cream or milk
1 egg yolk
salt and pepper

Set oven to 200°C (400°F), gas mark 6. Make a 20-cm (8-in) flan as described on page 19, adding the hot oil as soon as flan case comes out of the oven. Meanwhile fry the spring onions, lettuce and peas gently in the butter for 2–3 minutes. Remove from heat, mix in mint, cream, egg and seasoning; pour into flan case. Reduce oven setting to 190°C (375°F), gas mark 5. Bake for 30–35 minutes.

Marrow, Ginger and Cashew Nut Flan

An unusual late-summer flan with a pleasant tang.

SERVES 4–6

125 g (4 oz) shortcrust pastry
2 tablespoons oil
1 onion, chopped
25 g (1 oz) butter
450 g (1 lb) marrow, weighed after peeling and dicing
1 garlic clove, crushed
walnut-sized piece fresh ginger, grated
¼–½ teaspoon chilli powder
150 ml (5 fl oz) milk
1 egg
salt and pepper
50 g (2 oz) cashew nuts, chopped

Make a 20-cm (8-in) flan case as described on page 19, adding hot oil to baked flan case as explained. Fry onion in butter for 5 minutes. Add marrow, garlic, ginger and chilli and fry for 5–6 minutes. Spoon into flan case. Whisk milk and egg, add seasoning. Pour into flan, sprinkle with cashew nuts. Reduce oven setting to 190°C (375°F), gas mark 5. Bake for 35–40 minutes.

Flaky Mushroom Roll

This is good served with the soured cream and fresh herb sauce described on page 29.

SERVES 6 (F)

25 g (1 oz) butter
1 onion, chopped
2 garlic cloves, crushed
750 g (1½ lb) mushrooms, washed and chopped
2 tablespoons chopped parsley
125 g (4 oz) cooked brown rice
salt and pepper
200 g (8 oz) rough puff or cream cheese pastry
milk or beaten egg to glaze

Heat butter in a large saucepan and fry onion for 5 minutes; add garlic and mushrooms, cook for a further 20–35 minutes, until all liquid has boiled away. Remove from heat, add parsley, rice and seasoning. Cool. Set oven to 220°C (425°F), gas mark 7. Divide pastry in half, roll each into a rectangle 30 x 26 cm (12 x 10 in). Spoon mushroom mixture on to one half, dampen pastry edges. Cut second half as shown on page 28, place on top of mixture, press down. Place on baking sheet. Brush with glaze, bake for 30 minutes.

Mushroom Vol Au Vents

Serve these as a first course, or as a light lunch or supper, with ratatouille and a green salad.

MAKES 8, SERVES 4

250 g (9 oz) puff pastry
450 g (1 lb) button mushrooms, washed and chopped
25 g (1 oz) butter
2 teaspoons cornflour
275 ml (½ pint) milk or single cream
salt and pepper
grated nutmeg

Set oven to 200°C (400°F), gas mark 6. Using short strokes, in one direction only, roll pastry out 1 cm (½-in) thick. Cut into rounds with a lightly floured 5-cm (2-in) cutter. With a cutter one size smaller, mark each circle with another, inner circle. Place on a damp baking sheet; bake at top of oven for 30 minutes. Meanwhile fry mushrooms in butter for 5 minutes; add cornflour and cream, stir until thickened. Remove from heat; season. Remove tops of vol au vents, scoop out and discard inner pastry layers; fill with mushroom mixture. Reheat for 10–15 minutes before eating, but do not fill in advance or cases will go soggy.

Mushroom Flan

SERVES 4—6

125 g (4 oz) shortcrust pastry
2 tablespoons oil
1 onion, chopped
25 g (1 oz) butter
350 g (12 oz) button mushrooms, washed and chopped

1 small garlic clove, crushed
300 ml (11 fl oz) soured or single cream
2 egg yolks
salt and pepper
grated nutmeg
1 tablespoon chopped parsley

Set oven to 200°C (400°F), gas mark 6. Make a 20-cm (8-in) flan case according to instructions on page 19, adding hot oil to baked flan case as described. Fry onion in butter for 5 minutes, add mushrooms and garlic and cook until mushrooms are tender, 5–6 minutes. If mushrooms produce much liquid, continue to cook, uncovered, over a high heat until this has evaporated: this can take 20–30 minutes. Spoon mushroom mixture into flan case. Whisk cream and egg yolks, add seasoning, nutmeg and parsley. Pour over mushrooms. Reduce oven setting to 190°C (375°F), gas mark 5. Bake for 40–45 minutes.

Nutty Slice

This quick-to-make nourishing savoury pastry is good for picnics and lunch boxes.

SERVES 4

100 g (4 oz) Shortcrust or cream cheese pastry
2 tablespoons chutney or pickle
125 g (4 oz) peanuts: salted, or raw peanuts roasted in their skins for 10 minutes at 200°C (400°F), gas mark 6

1 onion, peeled
3 tomatoes, skinned
salt and pepper

Set oven to 220°C (425°F), gas mark 7. Roll pastry into a rectangle, spread with chutney. Blend peanuts, onion and tomatoes together in food processor; or grate or very finely chop peanuts and onion, chop tomato and mix together to make a paste. Spread mixture over half pastry, cover with other half. Press edges together, prick top. Place on baking sheet, bake for 30 minutes. Serve hot or cold, in slices.

Onion and Soured Cream Flan

SERVES 4-6

125 g (4 oz) shortcrust pastry
2 tablespoons oil
350 g (12 oz) onions, peeled and sliced
25 g (1 oz) butter
150 ml (5 fl oz) soured cream
2 egg yolks
salt and pepper
grated nutmeg

Set oven to 200°C (400°F), gas mark 6. Roll out pastry, line a 20-cm (8-in) flan tin, prick base. Bake at top of oven for 20 minutes. Heat oil in a small saucepan and as soon as flan case comes out of oven pour hot oil into base. Leave on one side. Meanwhile fry onion in butter until softened: 10 minutes. Cool slightly, then add cream, egg yolks, seasoning and nutmeg. Pour into flan case. Reduce oven setting to 180°C (350°F), gas mark 4. Bake flan in centre of oven for 35–40 minutes, until set.

Ratatouille Flan

This is good made with a shortcrust pastry flavoured with grated cheese: use 50–125 g (2–4 oz) cheese.

SERVES 4–6

125 g (4 oz) shortcrust pastry
4 tablespoons oil
1 onion, chopped
125 g (4 oz) aubergine, diced
125 g (4 oz) courgette, diced
1 small red pepper, de-seeded and chopped
1 garlic clove, crushed
2 tomatoes, skinned, de-seeded and chopped
150 ml (5 fl oz) soured cream
1 egg
salt and pepper

Make a 20-cm (8-in) flan case as described on page 19, adding hot oil to baked flan case as described. While flan case is cooking, fry onion in the oil for 5 minutes, then add aubergine, courgette, pepper and garlic and fry for a further 10 minutes. Add tomato, cream, egg and seasoning; spoon into flan case. Reduce oven setting to 190°C (375°F), gas mark 5. Bake flan in centre of oven for 35–40 minutes, until set.

aubergine = eggplant
courgette = little veg. marrow (or gourd or pumpkin)

Peanut, Ginger and Green Pepper Flan

I admit this is an unusual combination of ingredients, but it does work, resulting in a delicious flan.

SERVES 4–6

125 g (4 oz) wholewheat shortcrust pastry
4 tablespoons oil
1 onion, chopped
50 g (2 oz) green pepper, de-seeded and chopped
1 garlic clove, crushed
walnut-sized piece fresh ginger, grated
1 tomato, skinned, seeded and chopped
175g (6 oz) crunchy peanut butter
1 egg
salt and pepper

Make a 20-cm (8-in) flan case as described on page 19, heating 2 tablespoons of the oil and adding it to the baked flan case as described. Fry onion in the butter and remaining oil for 5 minutes, then add pepper, garlic, ginger and tomato and fry for a further 5–6 minutes. Remove from heat, mix in peanut butter, egg and seasoning. Spoon into flan case. Reduce oven setting to 190°C (375°F), gas mark 5. Bake for 25–30 minutes, until set.

Slimmer's Flan

Although pastry dishes are not normally considered 'slimming', this flan, cut into six pieces, contains only 270 calories a slice.

SERVES 4–6

100 g (4 oz) shortcrust pastry
2 tablespoons oil
50 g (2 oz) chopped spring onion
125 g (4 oz) carrots, coarsely grated
1 tablespoon chopped parsley
50 g (2 oz) grated cheese
6 tablespoons single cream
1 egg
salt and pepper

Set oven to 200°C (400°F), gas mark 6. Make a 20-cm (8-in) flan case as described on page 19, rolling pastry thinly, and adding hot oil to baked flan case as described. Mix together spring onion, carrot, parsley and cheese; spoon into flan case. Whisk cream and egg, add seasoning. Pour into flan case. Reduce oven setting to 190°C (375°F), gas mark 5. Bake flan in centre of oven for 30–35 minutes, until set.

Spinach, Almond and Cheese Flan

SERVES 4-6

100 g (4 oz) shortcrust pastry
2 tablespoons oil
450 g (1 lb) spinach
15 g (½-oz) butter
100 g (4 oz) split blanched almonds, toasted

75 g (3 oz) grated cheese
1 egg
salt and pepper

Set oven to 200°C (400°F), gas mark 6. Make a 20-cm (8-in) flan case as described on page 19, adding hot oil to baked flan case as described. Meanwhile cook spinach in a large saucepan without extra water for about 10 minutes. Drain and chop, then add butter, half almonds, half cheese, egg and seasoning. Mix well, then pour into flan case, spread top level and sprinkle with remaining cheese and almonds. Reduce oven setting to 190°C (375°F), gas mark 5. Bake flan in centre of oven for 35–40 minutes, until set.

Spinach Pie

This flaky golden pie makes a delicious first course or light lunch or supper dish, with a soured cream sauce (page 29) and salad or cooked vegetables.

SERVES 4–6 (F)

900 g (2 lb) fresh spinach or 450 g (1 lb) frozen
bunch spring onions, chopped
125 g (4 oz) feta or white Cheshire cheese, crumbled
salt and pepper
300 g (12 oz) flaky pastry
milk or beaten egg to glaze

Wash fresh spinach, cook in a large saucepan without extra water for about 10 minutes; cook frozen spinach according to instructions on packet. Drain and chop, add spring onions, cheese and seasoning, then leave until cold. Set oven to 200°C (400°F), gas mark 6. Roll out just over half of pastry and place in pie tin or dish. Put spinach mixture on top, moisten edge of pastry with cold water. Roll out rest of pastry to cover pie, press edges together, knock up and trim. Brush with glaze if liked. Bake for 40 minutes.

Quick Spring Onion Flan

Here is another speedily made flan, using spring onions which are quick to prepare and need no pre-cooking. If you've time to bake the flan case before adding the filling, of course it's crisper; but either way this flan is delicious served hot.

SERVES 4–6

100 g (4 oz) plain wholewheat flour	large bunch spring onions
pinch of salt	300 ml (11 fl oz) single or soured cream
50 g (2 oz) butter	2 egg yolks
1½ tablespoons water	salt and pepper

Set oven to 190°C (375°F), gas mark 5. Make pastry as described on page 8, roll out pastry, line a 20-cm (8-in) flan tin. Wash, trim and chop spring onions, place in flan. Whisk cream and egg yolks, add seasoning. Pour over spring onions. Bake flan in centre of oven for 45–50 minutes, until set. Serve at once.

Tomato Flan with Soured Cream and Basil

SERVES 4–6

450 g (1 lb) tomatoes, skinned, de-seeded and sliced
salt and pepper
100 g (4 oz) shortcrust pastry
2 tablespoons oil
1 tablespoon chopped basil
300 ml (11 fl oz) soured cream
2 egg yolks

Put the tomatoes into a sieve or colander, sprinkle with salt and pepper and leave on one side. Set oven to 200°C (400°F), gas mark 6. Roll out pastry, line a 20-cm (8-in) flan tin, prick base. Bake at top of oven for 20 minutes. Heat oil in a small saucepan and as soon as flan case comes out of oven pour hot oil into base. Arrange tomato slices in flan case, sprinkle with basil. Whisk cream and egg yolks, add seasoning, then pour over tomatoes. Reduce oven setting to 190°C (375°F), gas mark 5. Bake flan in centre of oven for 35–40 minutes, until set.

Vegetable Flan

SERVES 4–6

125 g (4 oz) wholewheat pastry
2 tablespoons oil
600 g (1¼ lb) mixed vegetables: carrot, courgette, onion, cauliflower, leek, as available, sliced
salt
25 g (1 oz) butter

25 g (1 oz) flour
300 ml (½ pint) milk
125 g (4 oz) grated cheese
½ teaspoon mustard powder
125 g (4 oz) button mushrooms, sliced
freshly ground pepper

Set oven to 200°C (400°F), gas mark 6. Make a 20-cm (8-in) flan case as described on page 19, adding hot oil to baked flan case as described. Cook vegetables in a little boiling salted water until just tender; drain. Melt butter in a pan, add flour, cook for 1–2 minutes, then add milk and stir over heat until thickened. Add half grated cheese, mustard, vegetables and mushrooms. Season, pile into flan case, sprinkle with rest of cheese. Bake for 20–25 minutes, until golden brown.

Vegetable and Butter Bean Pie with Flaky Crust

Serve this pie with mashed potatoes and a cooked green vegetable for an economical and delicious family meal.

SERVES 4–6 (F)

1 onion, chopped
25g (1 oz) butter
450g (1 lb) tomatoes, skinned and chopped
225 g (8 oz) carrots, scraped and sliced
350 g (12 oz) leeks, trimmed and sliced
125 g (4 oz) mushrooms
125 g (4 oz) butter beans, soaked and cooked,.or a 425-g (15-oz) can
salt and pepper
150 g (6 oz) flaky pastry
milk or beaten egg to glaze

Fry the onion in the butter for 5 minutes, then add the tomatoes, carrots, leeks and mushrooms and fry very gently for about 30 minutes, until vegetables are tender. Drain butter beans, add to mixture, together with seasoning. Spoon into 1-litre (1½–1¾ pint) pie dish, cool. Set oven to 220°C (425°F), gas mark 7. Roll pastry, place on top of pie dish, trim and finish as described on page 21. Bake pie for 30 minutes.

Walnut Pâté en Croute

SERVES 6 Ⓕ

50 g (2 oz) chopped onion
25 g (1 oz) chopped celery
15 g (½ oz) butter
1 garlic clove, crushed
50 g (2 oz) grated walnuts
175 g (6 oz) grated cashew nuts
125 g (4 oz) cooked mashed chestnuts
50 g (2 oz) grated cheese
1 egg, beaten
1 tablespoon brandy
pinch paprika
pinch thyme
salt and pepper
200 g (8 oz) flaky or cream cheese pastry
beaten egg to glaze

Fry onion and celery in butter for 10 minutes. Add garlic, nuts, cheese, egg, brandy, paprika, thyme and seasoning. Set oven to 220°C (425°F), gas mark 7. Roll half pastry into an oblong 30 x 26 cm (12 x 10 in). Spoon nut mixture on top, roll out second half, cut as shown on page 28, place on top. Brush with beaten egg. Bake for 30 minutes.

Index

Avocado flans, little 23

Brie, walnut and sorrel pies, little flaky 25
Butter bean
  onion and chutney roll 26
  pie with flaky crust, vegetable and 58

Cabbage, rice and hardboiled egg roll, flaky 29
Carrot, courgette and parsley flan 27
Cauliflower, Stilton and walnut flan 30
Cheese
  apple and sage turnovers 33
  and onion pie 31
  shortcrust 9
  and tomato flan, quick 34
Chick pea and potato pasties, spiced 37
Courgette and parsley flan, carrot 27
Cream cheese pastry 9
Curd cheese pies with spicy tomato sauce, little 35

Double crust pie, making a 18

Equipment 6–7

Fat 6
Flaky
  cabbage, rice and hardboiled egg roll 29
  mushroom roll 43
  pastry, 12–14
Flan
  carrot, courgette and parsley 27
  cauliflower, Stilton and walnut 30
  leek lattice 39
  lettuce, pea and spring onion 41

marrow, ginger and cashew
    nut 42
mushroom 46
onion and soured cream 48
peanut, ginger and green
    pepper 51
quick cheese and tomato 34
quick spring onion 55
ratatouille 49
slimmer's 52
spinach, almond and cheese 53
tomato with soured cream and
    basil 56
vegetable 57
Flans
  little avocado 23
  and tarts, making 19–20
Flour 5–6
Freezing pastry dishes 20

Ingredients for pastry 5–6
Introduction 5–7

Leek
  lattice flan 39
  pie 40
Lettuce, pea and spring onion
    flan 41

Liquids for pastry 6
Little
  avocado flans 23
  curd cheese pies with spicy
    tomato sauce 35
  flaky Brie, walnut and sorrel
    pies 25

Making the pastry 7
Marrow, ginger and cashew nut
  flan 42
Mushroom
  flan 46
  roll, flaky 43
  vol au vents 45

Nutty slice 47

Onion and soured cream flan 48

Pasties, spiced chick pea and
  potato 37
Pastry
  cheese shortcrust 9
  cream cheese 9
  equipment for 6–7
  flaky 12–14
  freezing 20

    ingredients for 5–6
    making the 7
    puff 14–17
    rough puff 11–12
    shortcrust 8
    types of 5
Peanut, ginger and green pepper flan 51
Pie
    cheese and onion 31
    double crust, making a 18
    leek 40
    single crust, making a 17
    spinach 54
    vegetable and butter bean, with flaky crust 58
Pies
    little curd cheese, with spicy tomato sauce 35
    little flaky Brie, walnut and sorrel 25
Puff pastry 14–17

Quiches, flans and tarts, making 19–20
Quick
    cheese and tomato flan 34
    spring onion flan 55

Ratatouille flan 49
Roll
    butter bean, onion and chutney 26
    flaky cabbage, rice and hardboiled egg 29
    flaky mushroom 43
Rough puff pastry 11–12

Shortcrust pastry 8
Single crust pie, making a 17
Slice, nutty 47
Slimmer's flan 52
Spiced chick pea and potato pasties 37
Spinach
    almond and cheese flan 53
    pie 54
Spring onion flan, quick 55

Tarts, making quiches, flans and 19–20
Tomato flan with soured cream and basil 56
Turnovers, cheese, apple and sage 33
Types of pastry 5

Vegetable
  and butter bean pie with flaky crust 58
  flan 57

Vol au vents, mushroom 45

Walnut
  flan, cauliflower, Stilton and 30
  pâté en croute 59